**Vocabulary Tests
Level 3**

**Suitable for ages 9 – 11**

Each word study unit contains

- Definition matching
- Cloze sentences

| **Contents** | | **Solutions** | |
|---|---|---|---|
| Unit 1 | page 2 | Unit 1 | page 42 |
| Unit 2 | page 4 | Unit 2 | page 42 |
| Unit 3 | page 6 | Unit 3 | page 42 |
| Unit 4 | page 8 | Unit 4 | page 43 |
| Unit 5 | page 10 | Unit 5 | page 43 |
| Unit 6 | page 12 | Unit 6 | page 44 |
| Unit 7 | page 14 | Unit 7 | page 44 |
| Unit 8 | page 16 | Unit 8 | page 44 |
| Unit 9 | page 18 | Unit 9 | page 45 |
| Unit 10 | page 20 | Unit 10 | page 45 |
| Test 1 | page 22 | Test 1 | page 46 |
| Test 2 | page 26 | Test 2 | page 47 |
| Test 3 | page 30 | Test 3 | page 48 |
| Test 4 | page 34 | Test 4 | page 49 |
| Test 5 | page 38 | Test 5 | page 50 |

Copyright © 2017 Simon Steggels
All rights reserved

No part of this book may be reproduced, stored in a retrieval system, communicated or transmitted in any form or by any means without prior written permission. All inquiries should be made to the publisher.

ISBN 978-0-6480967-7-1

Published by
Advanced Instruction Pty Ltd
www.advancedinstruction.com.au

# Unit 1

*Definitions—match the words in the bold with their meanings below*

| **lodge** | **glace** | **misfortune** | **distinct** |
|---|---|---|---|
| **quiver** | **moderate** | **dripping** | **poisonous** |
| **postpone** | **coax** | **miserable** | **parliament** |
| **refrigerate** | **decorate** | **torture** | **cartwheel** |

1. very wet _____

2. bad luck or an unlucky event _____

3. a small house in the country, used especially by people on holiday or taking part in sports _____

4. unpleasant and causing unhappiness _____

5. preserved in liquid sugar and then dried _____

6. to shake slightly due to strong emotion _____

7. very harmful and able to cause illness or death _____

8. neither small nor large in size, amount, degree, or strength _____

9. clearly noticeable, separate and different _____

10. to persuade someone gently to do something _____

11. to delay an event and plan that it should happen at a later date _____

12. the group of elected politicians or other people who make the laws for their country _____

13. a very unpleasant experience _____

14. to make or keep something cold so that it stays fresh _____

15. to make a place or thing more attractive _____

16. a fast skilful movement of the body in a sideways somersault, like a wheel turning _____

© MR STEGGELS ADVANCED INSTRUCTION PTY LTD

# Unit 1

*Word usage—complete the sentences using the words in bold from the previous page*

1. In Australia, _____ House is located in Canberra.

2. There has been a _____ improvement in Sam's attitude this year.

3. Can you tell the difference between edible and _____ mushrooms?

4. He found the two-hour violin recital sheer _____ to listen to as he preferred loud rock concerts.

5. You must _____ fresh orange juice and drink it within three days.

6. We will _____ the hall with orange streamers for Harmony Day.

7. Breaking both legs in the accident was a terrible _____ for the athlete.

8. Due to family problems, they decided to _____ their holiday until May.

9. After a huge snowfall, the family was stranded at the ski _____.

10. Jim had just been on a run and was _____ with sweat.

11. Turning down the lights sent a _____ of excitement through the audience.

12. Perhaps you could _____ your father into taking us to the movies.

13. The recipe required one half cup of _____ cherries.

14. The _____ weather meant that sport was cancelled.

15. There has been a _____ improvement in my health since I began yoga.

16. The gymnast demonstrated how to perform a _____.

# Unit 2

*Definitions—match the words in the bold with their meanings below*

| **accent** | **aquatic** | **rip-off** | **scrawl** |
| **suppressed** | **vocalise** | **passage** | **territory** |
| **gawking** | **secretion** | **gross** | **drab** |
| **slunk** | **stubby** | **moral** | **visual pollution** |

1. short and thick
2. an area that an animal tries to control or thinks belongs to them
3. prevented something from being seen or expressed
4. untidy writing that is difficult to read
5. the way in which people in a particular area, country, or social group pronounce words
6. a usually long and narrow part of a building with rooms on one or both sides, or a covered path that connects places
7. extremely unpleasant, revolting
8. something that is not worth what you pay for it
9. the message that you understand from a story about how you should or should not behave
10. to express feelings or ideas in words or sounds
11. liquid produced by an animal or plant
12. staring at something or someone in a stupid or rude way
13. boring, especially in appearance; having little colour and excitement
14. living or growing in, happening in, or connected with water
15. the presence of any unwanted sight that can ruin the appeal of an area
16. walked away from somewhere quietly and unnoticed

© MR STEGGELS ADVANCED INSTRUCTION PTY LTD

# Unit 2

*Word usage—complete the sentences using the words in bold from the previous page*

1. He _____ out of the room to avoid getting into trouble.

2. I like to grow _____ plants in my backyard pond.

3. _____ is especially noticeable in city and urban areas.

4. 'Don't stand there _____ ,' she said. 'Help me with this heavy pot!'

5. The concrete buildings looked _____ in the rain.

6. Even though she is French, she speaks with an impeccable English _____.

7. I _____ my anger and simply smiled at the rude customer.

8. The robin keeps other birds away from the garden – it's his _____.

9. '$300 for a t-shirt?' I cried. 'That's a total _____!'

10. He had _____ fingers so he couldn't play the piano very well.

11. The excessive _____ of gastric juices in the gut causes ulcers.

12. 'I hope you can read my _____,' the boy said to his teacher.

13. 'Oh, _____!' I cried, pointing at the cockroach crawling over the food.

14. The _____ of this story is that honesty is always the best policy.

15. Most people find it hard to _____ their fears.

16. A narrow _____ led directly through the house into the garden.

# Unit 3

*Definitions—match the words in the bold with their meanings below*

| billowing | foghorn | eccentricity | discoveries |
| whimper | virtually | in spite | intact |
| spluttering | hardened | annoyance | expedition |
| timber | petition | coyly | foothills |

1. low mountains at the bottom of a larger mountain  _____
2. spread over a large area, to become filled with air  _____
3. the state of being strange or unusual, in a humorous way  _____
4. to make a series of small, weak sounds that express unhappiness  _____
5. a document signed by a large number of people demanding or asking for some action from the government  _____
6. almost  _____
7. wood used for building  _____
8. used before one fact that makes another fact surprising  _____
9. not likely to change a bad way of life or feel sorry about it  _____
10. the feeling or state of being angry  _____
11. speaking in a quick and confused way, producing short, unclear noises because of surprise or anger  _____
12. an organised journey for a particular purpose  _____
13. information, places, objects found for the first time  _____
14. complete and in the original state  _____
15. acting in a way to intentionally keep something secret  _____
16. a horn that makes a very loud sound to warn ships that they are close to land or other ships  _____

# Unit 3

*Word usage—complete the sentences using the words in bold from the previous page*

1. The nature reserve is located in the _____ of the Pyrenees.

2. The child began to _____ when his ice cream fell on the floor.

3. The tomato sauce stain on my shirt has _____ disappeared.

4. He has an unpleasantly loud voice; he sounds like a _____.

5. I was _____ with anger when I found graffiti all over the walls my apartment block.

6. We watched the yachts on the harbour with their _____ sails.

7. When asked her age, she replied _____, 'How old do you think I am?'

8. _____ of his injury, he will play in the grand final.

9. She is known for her _____ and often wears a top hat to go shopping.

10. I can understand your _____ at having to wait for six hours to see a doctor.

11. Leonardo da Vinci made many scientific _____.

12. The church was destroyed in the bombing but the altar remains _____.

13. I signed a _____ against the proposed closure of the local hospital.

14. These trees are being grown for _____ and will be used to make frames for houses.

15. Only the most _____ criminals are sent to Lone Pike Prison.

16. The explorer died while he was on an _____ in the Antarctic.

© MR STEGGELS ADVANCED INSTRUCTION PTY LTD

**Unit 4**

*Definitions—match the words in the bold with their meanings below*

| inhospitable | friction | empire | colourless |
| geological | lever | granary | pioneer |
| crevasse | experiment | dynasty | granite |
| rations | gigantic | yield | presto |

1. a deep, narrow opening or crack in an area of thick ice or rock  _____
2. a test or trial for the purpose of discovering something unknown  _____
3. a bar or handle that moves around a point, so that one end of it can be pushed or pulled  _____
4. describes the physical processes of the earth in order to understand its origin and history  _____
5. very large in size, extent, or amount  _____
6. not suitable for humans to live in  _____
7. a building for storing grain  _____
8. total amount of food that is given to someone to be eaten during a particular activity and in a particular period of time  _____
9. to give up under pressure; surrender  _____
10. a group of countries ruled by a single person, government, or country  _____
11. fast tempo  _____
12. a succession of powerful leaders all from the same family  _____
13. the force that makes it difficult for one object to slide along the surface of another  _____
14. hard grey, pink, black light-colored rock that is used for building and monuments  _____
15. not exciting or interesting  _____
16. the first person to do something  _____

© MR STEGGELS ADVANCED INSTRUCTION PTY LTD

# Unit 4

*Word usage—complete the sentences using the words in bold from the previous page*

1. The Ming _____ lasted for over two hundred and fifty years.

2. One slip and the mountaineers would fall into the _____ and die.

3. Scientists conducted a _____ survey of the coastline.

4. During the war, _____ of food, clothing and fuel were strict.

5. The climbers had to trek for miles through _____ countryside.

6. The farm features a large _____ and a wool warehouse.

7. The Roman _____ existed from 27 BC to 476 AD.

8. The _____ wave increased in height as it sped toward the coast.

9. When you rub your hands together, _____ produces heat.

10. 'You will _____ to me!' cried the evil wizard, as he stood over the injured prince.

11. The students performed an _____ to show the class that air is heavy.

12. A wheelbarrow is an example of the simple machine called a _____.

13. *The Boston Newsletter* was the _____ of the American press.

14. On rainy days in winter, the city is cold and _____.

15. 'Hey _____!' said the magician, as he pulled a rabbit out of his hat.

16. The beautiful _____ structure of East Station was completed in 1888 and, within six years, became the busiest train station in the country.

**Unit 5**

*Definitions—match the words in the bold with their meanings below*

| despise | corral | underway | rhomboid |
|---|---|---|---|
| abandon | amid | exports | hexagonal |
| admiration | proclaim | protestor | parallel |
| fare | steers | tournament | horizontal |

1. in the middle of or surrounded by  _____
2. young male cattle that have had their sex organs removed, usually kept for meat  _____
3. to feel a strong dislike for someone or something  _____
4. an area surrounded by a fence for keeping horses or cattle  _____
5. products that you sell to another country  _____
6. to leave a place, thing, or person, usually forever  _____
7. someone who shows that they disagree with something by standing somewhere, shouting and carrying signs  _____
8. to succeed or to perform in a stated way in a particular situation  _____
9. a competition for teams or single players in which winners play against each other until only one is left  _____
10. respect and approval of someone or their behaviour  _____
11. happening now  _____
12. a type of flat shape with four equal straight sides  _____
13. to announce something publicly or officially, especially something positive  _____
14. describes a two dimensional, six-sided shape  _____
15. along the plane of the horizon, at right angles to vertical  _____
16. distance between lines is the same all along their length  _____

# Unit 5

*Word usage—complete the sentences using the words in bold from the previous page*

1. Keep the injured cyclist _____ with his feet slightly raised.

2. Unfortunately, we were defeated in the first round of the _____ .

3. Hills Road runs _____ to Mill Road so they do not meet.

4. It is common knowledge that the rival teams _____ each other.

5. The building was similar to a beehive as it was _____ in shape.

6. Opposite sides are equal and opposite angles are equal in a _____ .

7. The girl's mother asked her, 'How did you _____ in your exams?'

8. The cattle dog rounded up the herd of cattle and directed it to the _____ .

9. We were sinking fast so the captain gave the order to _____ ship.

10. The Prime Minister stated that economic recovery was already _____ .

11. Doctors and nurses who work in war zones are worthy of our _____ .

12. Brazil plans to increase its coffee _____ over the next five years.

13. _____ are used to run beside the bulls and direct them toward the gate.

14. The candidate will _____ victory before all votes have been counted.

15. Police had to arrest the _____ after she smashed a shop window.

16. On the floor, _____ mounds of books, Sam found the treasure map.

© MR STEGGELS ADVANCED INSTRUCTION PTY LTD

# Unit 6

*Definitions—match the words in the bold with their meanings below*

| plague | campaign | part-time | breakneck |
| dreary | semi-precious | bellowed | destination |
| diehard | enhance | supposed | motorway |
| lyrics | deposed | poked | records |

1. to improve the quality, amount, or strength of something _____
2. a wide road for fast-moving traffic, with a limited number of places at which drivers can enter and leave _____
3. to have a duty or a responsibility to do something _____
4. boring and making you feel unhappy _____
5. carelessly fast and dangerous speed _____
6. work for only some of the day or the week _____
7. to cause worry or difficulty to someone over a period of time _____
8. pushed a finger quickly into someone or something _____
9. the words of a song _____
10. a planned group of political, business, or military activities _____
11. the best or fastest things ever done _____
12. the place where someone or something is going _____
13. a stone used in jewellery but not really valuable _____
14. shouted in a loud voice _____
15. removed someone important from a powerful position _____
16. unwilling to change your support for someone or something even when many others disagree _____

# Unit 6

*Word usage—complete the sentences using the words in bold from the previous page*

1. Adding butter to the chicken casserole will _____ the flavour.

2. After my children were born, I decided to go back to work _____.

3. The boys had to spend another _____ day inside while the rain fell.

4. 'Sit down and eat your lunch!' the teacher _____ across playground.

5. Only a _____ supporter would still follow a losing football team.

6. Workers are _____ to be in the office by 8.45 a.m.

7. Health problems will _____ you if you take on too much work.

8. You almost _____ me in the eye with that umbrella!

9. The choir had to memorise the _____ of the song for the recital.

10. King Charles I was _____ from the English throne in 1646.

11. The Prime Minister was busy preparing his election _____.

12. He ran the 100 metres in 9.79 seconds and broke the Olympic and World _____.

13. Jade and turquoise are _____ stones.

14. Due to the bad weather, conditions on the _____ are hazardous.

15. We finally arrived at our _____, tired and hungry.

16. They motorcyclists were racing at _____ speed.

© MR STEGGELS ADVANCED INSTRUCTION PTY LTD

# Unit 7

*Definitions—match the words in the bold with their meanings below*

| | | | |
|---|---|---|---|
| **lantern** | **broadcast** | **quilt** | **gorgeous** |
| **gossamer** | **pitch** | **budget** | **oafish** |
| **sapphire** | **commentator** | **thundercloud** | **Dutch** |
| **dew** | **insist** | **kiddo** | **scoundrel** |

1. drops of water that form outside during the night  _____

2. very beautiful  _____

3. delicate and light  _____

4. a decorative cover for a bed  _____

5. a light inside a container that has a handle  _____

6. the amount of money you have available to spend  _____

7. a friendly form of address  _____

8. a precious stone, usually bright blue, often used in jewellery  _____

9. a person, especially a man, who treats other people very badly  _____

10. from the Netherlands  _____

11. to send out a program on television or radio  _____

12. to say firmly especially when others disagree with you  _____

13. stupid, rude or awkward  _____

14. an area painted with lines for playing particular sports  _____

15. a large, dark cloud that produces thunder and lightning  _____

16. a reporter for radio or television who provides a spoken description of and remarks on an event  _____

© MR STEGGELS ADVANCED INSTRUCTION PTY LTD

# Unit 7

*Word usage—complete the sentences using the words in bold from the previous page*

1. The _____ man burped loudly in front of guests at the dinner table.

2. _____ is the language spoken by 20 million people in the Netherlands.

3. Our teacher wears a ring with a large _____.

4. The heartless _____ stole the old lady's handbag, knocking her over.

5. A _____ drifted over the park, dropping torrents of rain.

6. On Halloween, I place a _____ carved from a pumpkin, at the front door.

7. The intricate patchwork _____ that my grandmother had hand sewn, was a family heirloom.

8. The bride wore a _____ veil.

9. The radio _____ announced that Australia had beaten New Zealand in the final of the Netball World Championships.

10. When we awoke at 6am, the ground outside out tent was covered with _____.

11. Supporters invaded the _____ as soon as the game ended.

12. The suspect will _____ on seeing her lawyer the moment she is arrested.

13. The company has drawn up a _____ for the coming financial year.

14. The tennis championship is _____ live to several different countries.

15. The sun was shining and their was a light breeze; it was a _____ day!

16. 'Come on, _____ ,' said my coach. 'Time to practise your pitching.'

© MR STEGGELS ADVANCED INSTRUCTION PTY LTD

# Unit 8

*Definitions—match the words in the bold with their meanings below*

| incentive | lavish | attic | region |
| discipline | guillotine | harpsichord | resistance |
| minister | affair | renowned | Asia-Pacific |
| disgusted | hoarding | loft | chameleon |

1. large in quantity and expensive or impressive  _____
2. the space or room at the top of a building, under the roof  _____
3. to teach someone to behave in a controlled way  _____
4. a device, invented in France, consisting of a sharp blade in a tall frame used to remove someone's head  _____
5. famous for something  _____
6. something that encourages a person to do something  _____
7. a particular area or part of the world, or any of the large official areas into which a country is divided  _____
8. an upper floor  _____
9. the part of the world in or near the Western Pacific Ocean  _____
10. a member of the government in charge of a particular department  _____
11. the act of fighting against something that is attacking you, or refusing to accept something  _____
12. a lizard that can change its skin colour according to its environment  _____
13. collecting large amounts of something to keep in a safe, often secret place  _____
14. a musical instrument similar to a piano played especially in the 17th and 18th centuries  _____
15. felt extreme dislike or disapproval of something  _____
16. a matter or situation that causes strong public feeling, usually of moral disapproval  _____

# Unit 8

*Word usage—complete the sentences using the words in bold from the previous page*

1. The _____ hid from the predator by turning leaf-green.

2. I am trying to _____ myself to eat less chocolate.

3. Bonus payments provide workers with an _____ to work harder.

4. This region of France is _____ for its outstanding natural beauty.

5. I own a _____ apartment; my bedroom is located above the living room.

6. The foreign _____ announced a new trading agreement with China.

7. I have boxes of old clothes stored in the _____.

8. The president's handling of the secret _____ has been widely criticised.

9. Mrs Brown said she was totally _____ with my behaviour today after I ruined the class play by storming off stage.

10. Mozart was especially skilled at playing the _____.

11. There would be enough food for everyone if people were not _____ it.

12. There's a shortage of sugar cane in the tropical _____.

13. Government troops offered no _____ to rebel forces.

14. King Louis XVI and Marie Antoinette faced the _____ during the French Revolution.

15. The evening was a _____ affair with glorious food.

16. The _____ region includes Southeast Asia and Oceania.

© MR STEGGELS ADVANCED INSTRUCTION PTY LTD

# Unit 9

*Definitions—match the words in the bold with their meanings below*

| converted | upturned | engineering | protective |
| devote | scrambled | ventilation | banned |
| series | murky | route | barriers |
| dedicated | obviously | freight | travelling |

1. gave all of your energy and time to a job or task
2. ensuring that someone or something is safe from harm
3. the work in designing and building machines and structures, and the study of this field
4. the part that is usually at the bottom is now at the top
5. dark and dirty or difficult to see through, especially water
6. in a way that is easy to understand or clear see
7. changed into a new form
8. goods that are carried from one place to another, by ship, aircraft, train, or truck
9. a set of books published by one author on the same subject
10. the movement of fresh air around a closed space
11. moving from one place to another
12. a particular path
13. fences or walls that stop people from going somewhere
14. moved or climbed quickly but with difficulty, using your hands to help you
15. not allowed
16. to give all of your time, effort, or love, or yourself, to something you believe in or to another person

# Unit 9

*Word usage—complete the sentences using the words in bold from the previous page*

1. The new principal _____ herself to improving the students' results.

2. The warehouse has been _____ into apartments with high ceilings.

3. The river was brown and _____ after the storm.

4. I missed the third episode of the _____ so I can't follow the plot now.

5. He has a new job overseas, so he is always _____.

6. _____, a factory cannot function without workers.

7. Special steel _____ have been erected all along the parade route.

8. I left a stressful job to _____ more time to my family.

9. An _____ boat on the beach provided shelter from the savage sun.

10. The woman _____ up the steep hillside and over the rocks.

11. My brother studies _____ at university.

12. The bedroom had poor _____ and in summer it became too hot.

13. I live on a bus _____ so it's quite easy for me to get to work.

14. Because his behaviour was so bad, the boy was _____ from school camps for the next two years.

15. When I paint the house, I always wear a _____ mask and goggles.

16. The large ship carries both _____ and passengers.

# Unit 10

*Definitions—match the words in the bold with their meanings below*

| fasting | flywire | toxin | developed |
| abundant | glinting | antidote | obese |
| drastically | dislodged | paralysis | digest |
| devastating | pride and joy | fluorescent | cells |

1. something or someone that you are very proud of _____
2. eating little or no food for a period of time _____
3. available in large quantities so that there is more than enough _____
4. a poisonous substance that causes diseases _____
5. shining brightly with a flash of light _____
6. in a way that is extreme and sudden _____
7. thin sheet of mesh over windows and doors for keeping out insects _____
8. a substance that stops the effects of a poison _____
9. forced or knocked something out of its position _____
10. colours that are very bright and easy to see, even in the dark _____
11. the smallest parts of a living thing that can exist _____
12. one of the rich countries of the world with many industries and comfortable living for most people _____
13. the loss of the ability to move all or part of your body _____
14. badly damaging or destroying something _____
15. very fat in a way that is unhealthy _____
16. to change food that you have eaten into substances that your body can use _____

# Unit 10

*Word usage—complete the sentences using the words in bold from the previous page*

1. Our red blood _____ deliver oxygen to the body's tissues.

2. I _____ a large rock as I climbed up the hill, and lost my footing.

3. _____ is part of many religions.

4. There is an _____ supply of fresh water in our lakes.

5. Our new grandson is our _____.

6. The size of the army was _____ cut to save money elsewhere.

7. If a snake bites you, the _____ will spread quickly throughout your body.

8. There is no known _____ to a bite from this snake.

9. The snake's poison causes _____.

10. Sunlight was _____ off the windows of a tall apartment building.

11. The colour of the strange creature was _____ orange.

12. The oil spill had a _____ effect on wildlife.

13. The charity works with poor children in less _____ countries.

14. If you don't exercise, and always eat fatty foods, you will become _____.

15. The _____ on our front door screen needed to be replaced.

16. Humans can _____ a wide range of food easily.

© MR STEGGELS ADVANCED INSTRUCTION PTY LTD

# Test 1

1. Which word means **the way in which people in a particular area pronounce words?**

    A   vocalise
    B   proclaim
    C   accent
    D   converted

2. Choose the best meaning of the word **amid**

    A   clearly noticeable, separate and different
    B   fast tempo
    C   happening now
    D   in the middle of or surrounded by

3. Choose the word that is closest in meaning to **fare**

    A   perform
    B   compete
    C   surrender
    D   survive

4. Choose the word that is most opposite in meaning to **murky**

    A   difficult
    B   dark
    C   clear
    D   fresh

5. The letters in **droelsunc** can be rearranged to make a word meaning

    A   shouted in a loud voice
    B   a person, especially a man, who treats other people very badly
    C   very beautiful
    D   a lizard that can change its skin colour according to its environment

6. Choose the word that best completes the sentence

   The tiny boat was _____ by a large wave.

   A   upturned
   B   abandoned
   C   aquatic
   D   dislodged

7. The letters in **taaunndb** can be rearranged to make a word meaning

   A   to leave a place, thing, or person, usually for ever
   B   badly damaging or destroying something
   C   forced or knocked something out of its position
   D   available in large quantities so that there is more than enough

8. Which pair of words is closest in meaning?

   A   devote         dedicate
   B   scrambled      dislodged
   C   renowned       abandoned
   D   region         geological

9. Which pair of words is most opposite in meaning?

   A   glinting       fluorescent
   B   barriers       banned
   C   yield          resist
   D   stubby         murky

10. Which word should replace the words in bold in the following sentence?

    Jim **felt a strong dislike for** Adam after he stole his expensive bike and sold it for $50.

    A   banned
    B   admired
    C   suppressed
    D   despised

11. Which is green in colour?

    A   sapphire
    B   granite
    C   gossamer
    D   none of the above

12. A **tournament** is also called a

    A   broadcast
    B   winner
    C   campaign
    D   competition

13. Which word means **the words of a song**?

    A   lyrics
    B   vocalise
    C   records
    D   pitch

14. Choose the word that is most similar in meaning to **moral**

    A   plague
    B   message
    C   moderate
    D   deposed

15. Choose the words that best complete the sentence

    He drove down the _____ at _____ speed.

    A   foothills       particular
    B   destination     protective
    C   motorway        breakneck
    D   flywire         devastating

© MR STEGGELS ADVANCED INSTRUCTION PTY LTD

16. Choose the word that best completes the sentence

The _____ was directly above and behind the kitchen with no privacy screen, so it wasn't the best place for a bedroom.

A  attic
B  loft
C  barrier
D  none of the above

17. The letters in **rodserc** can be rearranged to make a word meaning

A  boring and making you feel unhappy
B  to improve the quality, amount, or strength of something
C  the best or fastest things ever done
D  someone who is unwilling to change

18. Which pair of words is closest in meaning?

A  hoarding    dripping
B  flywire     ventilation
C  territory   region
D  miserable   misfortune

19. Choose the best definition of the word **eccentricity**

A  acting in a way to intentionally keep something secret
B  the state of being strange or unusual, in a humorous way
C  not likely to change a bad way of life or feel sorry about it
D  respect and approval of someone or their behaviour

20. Which word should replace the words in bold in the following sentence?

The bus followed a **particular path** on its way from the city to the beach.

A  expedition
B  destination
C  travelling
D  route

© MR STEGGELS ADVANCED INSTRUCTION PTY LTD

**Test 2**

1. Which word means **liquid produced by an animal or plant**?

    A    glace
    B    secretion
    C    slunk
    D    digest

2. Choose the best meaning of the word **intact**

    A    complete and in the original state
    B    spread over a large area, to become filled with air
    C    very large in size, extent, or amount
    D    to improve the quality, amount, or strength of something

3. Choose the word that is closest in meaning to **gawking**

    A    rude
    B    stupid
    C    travelling
    D    staring

4. Choose the word that is most opposite in meaning to **gigantic**

    A    obese
    B    billowing
    C    stubby
    D    lavish

5. The letters in **slecouorsl** can be rearranged into a word meaning

    A    bad luck or an unlucky event
    B    not exciting or interesting
    C    stupid, rude or awkward
    D    none of the above

© MR STEGGELS ADVANCED INSTRUCTION PTY LTD

6. Choose the word that best completes the sentence

   _____ lights are very bright so they are often used in offices.

   A   Glinting
   B   Lavish
   C   Semi-precious
   D   Fluorescent

7. The letters in **yaanrrg** can be rearranged to make a word meaning

   A   an organised journey for a particular purpose
   B   very large in size, extent, or amount
   C   not suitable for humans to live in
   D   a building for storing grain

8. Which pair of words is closest in meaning?

   A   drab        dreary
   B   obviously   coyly
   C   moderate    decorate
   D   affair      moral

9. Which pair of words is most opposite in meaning?

   A   dedicated   despised
   B   breakneck   guillotine
   C   poison      antidote
   D   insist      digest

10. Which word should replace the words in bold in the following sentence?

    Our teacher offered free time as **something that encouraged us** to work harder.

    A   petition
    B   torture
    C   discipline
    D   incentive

11. Choose the best word to complete the sentence

    _____ of our best efforts, we have been unable to contact the winner of last week's lottery draw.

    A   In spite
    B   Hardened
    C   Particular
    D   none of the above

12. A **chameleon** is a

    A   young, male cow kept mainly for meat
    B   decorative cover for a bed
    C   stone used in making jewellery
    D   lizard that can change colour

13. Which word means **in way that is extreme and sudden**?

    A   devastating
    B   misfortune
    C   drastically
    D   virtually

14. Choose the word that is most similar in meaning to **gross**

    A   drab
    B   obese
    C   poisonous
    D   none of the above

15. Which is the odd word out?

    A   hexagonal
    B   lever
    C   horizontal
    D   parallel

© MR STEGGELS ADVANCED INSTRUCTION PTY LTD

16. Choose the words that best complete the sentence

    It would be hours before the _____ reached its _____.

    A   expedition    region
    B   freight       destination
    C   exports       motorway
    D   broadcast     commentator

17. The letters in **bndean** can be rearranged to make a word meaning

    A   giving protection
    B   in a way that is easy to understand or see
    C   not allowed
    D   the movement of fresh air around a closed space

18. Which pair of words is most opposite in meaning?

    A   protective    oafish
    B   obviously     virtually
    C   rations       digest
    D   underway      postponed

19. Which is a device, invented in France, consisting of a sharp blade in a tall frame used to remove someone's head?

    A   glace
    B   gossamer
    C   guillotine
    D   harpsichord

20. Which word should replace the words in bold in the following sentence?

    India was ruled by a **succession of powerful leaders** started by the Mogul family.

    A   empire
    B   dynasty
    C   discipline
    D   parliament

© MR STEGGELS ADVANCED INSTRUCTION PTY LTD

**Test 3**

1. Which word means **fast tempo?**

    A   pitch
    B   presto
    C   pioneer
    D   none of the above

2. Choose the best meaning of the word **ventilation**

    A   respect and approval of someone or their behaviour
    B   the loss of the ability to move all or part of your body
    C   moving from one place to another
    D   the movement of fresh air around a closed space

3. Choose the word that is closest in meaning to **obviously**

    A   virtually
    B   coyly
    C   drastically
    D   clearly

4. Choose the word that is most opposite in meaning to **renowned**

    A   unknown
    B   undeveloped
    C   enhanced
    D   famous

5. Another word for **oafish** is

    A   rude
    B   stupid
    C   awkward
    D   all of the above

© MR STEGGELS ADVANCED INSTRUCTION PTY LTD

6. Choose the word that best completes the sentence

   When the bell went, the students _____ out of the classroom.

   A   converted
   B   scrambled
   C   scrawled
   D   dislodged

7. The letters in **canehen** can be rearranged to make a word meaning

   A   to improve the quality, amount, or strength of something
   B   to have a duty or a responsibility to do something
   C   boring and making you feel unhappy
   D   carelessly fast and dangerous

8. Which word should replace the words in bold in the following sentence?

   Sir Isaac Newton was a **person to discover many things before others** in the field of science.

   A   protestor
   B   commentator
   C   pioneer
   D   minister

9. Choose the best word to complete the sentence

   Red blood _____ remove carbon dioxide from your body.

   A   exports
   B   barriers
   C   cells
   D   secretions

10. Which word should replace the words in bold in the following sentence?

    The explorers set out on an **organised journey for a particular purpose** across Red Mountain.

    A   motorway
    B   expedition
    C   experiment
    D   corral

© MR STEGGELS ADVANCED INSTRUCTION PTY LTD

11. Choose the best word to complete the sentence

   To my great _____, the roast dinner I had ordered was served cold.

   A   incentive
   B   resistance
   C   paralysis
   D   annoyance

12. Which would most likely cause **disease**?

   A   an antidote
   B   fasting
   C   a toxin
   D   an affair

13. Which of the following has **four sides**?

   A   rhomboid
   B   hexagon
   C   parallel
   D   horizontal

14. What is the best definition of **visual pollution**?

   A   untidy writing that is difficult to read
   B   the message that you understand from a story about how you should or should not behave
   C   the presence of any unwanted sight that can ruin the appeal of an area
   D   none of the above

15. Which of the following is grey, pink or black in colour?

   A   attic
   B   thundercloud
   C   cells
   D   granite

© MR STEGGELS ADVANCED INSTRUCTION PTY LTD

16. Choose the word that best completes the sentence

He was in the _____, teaching his new horse to jump.

- A     corral
- B     pitch
- C     crevasse
- D     lodge

17. The letters in **loveeeddp** can be rearranged to make a word meaning

- A     something or someone that you are very proud of
- B     describes one of the rich countries of the world
- C     forced or knocked something out of its position
- D     very fat in a way that is unhealthy

18. Which is most likely to start a **petition**?

- A     a commentator
- B     a pioneer
- C     a minister
- D     a protestor

19. Choose the best definition of the word **plague**

- A     to fight against something that is attacking you
- B     to collect large amounts of something and keep it in a safe, often secret, place
- C     to cause worry or difficulty to someone over a period of time
- D     to remove someone important from a powerful position

20. Which word should replace the words in bold in the following sentence?

The wet weather is **unpleasant and causing unhappiness** for all of the children at camp.

- A     moderate
- B     dripping
- C     aquatic
- D     miserable

© MR STEGGELS ADVANCED INSTRUCTION PTY LTD

**Test 4**

1. Which word means **prevented something from being seen or expressed**?

    A   suppressed
    B   devote
    C   disgusted
    D   hardened

2. Choose the best meaning of the word **slunk**

    A   preserved in liquid sugar and then dried
    B   acting in a way to intentionally keep something secret
    C   walked away from somewhere quietly and unnoticed
    D   none of the above

3. Which pair is most similar in meaning?

    A   loft         ventilation
    B   lantern      fluorescent
    C   admiration   destination
    D   freight      exports

4. Which is most opposite in meaning to **paralysis**?

    A   travelling
    B   movement
    C   stomped
    D   antidote

5. Choose the words that best complete the sentence

    The _____ had to be _____ due to poor weather.

    A   harpsichord   dedicated
    B   experiment    deposed
    C   tournament    postponed
    D   granary       upturned

© MR STEGGELS ADVANCED INSTRUCTION PTY LTD

6. Choose the word that best completes the sentence

   He was _____ king after the death of his father, Barnaby VII.

   A   dedicated
   B   devoted
   C   proclaimed
   D   empire

7. The letters in **resets** can be rearranged to make a word meaning

   A   young male cattle that have had their sex organs removed, usually kept for meat
   B   to succeed or to perform in a stated way in a particular situation
   C   happening now
   D   to feel a strong dislike for someone or something

8. Which word should replace the words in bold in the following sentence?

   The general will lead a **planned group of military activities** to take control of enemy territory.

   A   parliament
   B   protest
   C   campaign
   D   none of the above

9. Choose the best meaning of the word **barriers**

   A   a particular path
   B   not allowed
   C   giving protection
   D   fences or walls that stop people from going somewhere

10. Which word should replace the words in bold in the following sentence?

    The active volcano made the region **not suitable for humans to live in**.

    A   banned
    B   inhospitable
    C   devastating
    D   poisonous

© MR STEGGELS ADVANCED INSTRUCTION PTY LTD

11. Which word refers to **a deep, narrow opening or crack in an area of thick ice or rock**?

    A   geological
    B   friction
    C   crevasse
    D   route

12. Which is a course that a student might study at university?

    A   engineering
    B   discoveries
    C   geological
    D   parliament

13. Which of the following is a natural force?

    A   ventilation
    B   thundercloud
    C   friction
    D   fly wire

14. Which word should replace the words in bold in the following sentence?

    The scientists will conduct **a test or trial** for the purpose of discovering more about gravity.

    A   an expedition
    B   a protest
    C   an experiment
    D   none of the above

15. Which of the following describes someone who is **unwilling to change their support even when many others disagree**?

    A   renowned
    B   hardened
    C   commentator
    D   diehard

© MR STEGGELS ADVANCED INSTRUCTION PTY LTD

16. Choose the words that best complete the sentence

    When war broke out, _____ reduced and many people went hungry.

    A   hoarding was
    B   resistance was
    C   exports were
    D   rations were

17. The letters in **dopseed** can be rearranged to make a word meaning

    A   very large in size, extent, or amount
    B   to have a duty or a responsibility to do something
    C   removed someone important from a powerful position
    D   none of the above

18. Which is best for managing your money effectively?

    A   budget
    B   rip-off
    C   incentive
    D   rations

19. Which is an example of a **lever**?

    A   attic
    B   lantern
    C   timber
    D   wheelbarrow

20. Choose the word that best completes the sentence

    The New Year celebrations get _____ at 9pm with the kids' fireworks display.

    A   grueling
    B   underway
    C   complex
    D   extinct

© MR STEGGELS ADVANCED INSTRUCTION PTY LTD

**Test 5**

1. Which word means **to have a duty or a responsibility to do something**?

   A  supposed
   B  suppressed
   C  virtually
   D  insist

2. Choose the best meaning of the word **poked**

   A  removed someone important from a powerful position
   B  gave up under pressure; surrender
   C  pushed a finger quickly into someone
   D  prevented something from being seen or expressed

3. **Hoarding** is

   A  giving protection
   B  badly damaging or destroying something
   C  fighting against something that is attacking you, or refusing to accept something
   D  collecting large amounts of something to keep in a safe, often secret place

4. When someone is **fasting**, they are

   A  changing food that they have eaten into substances that the body can use
   B  shining brightly with a flash of light
   C  eating little or no food for a period of time
   D  moving quickly from one place to another

5. The letters in **soorugge** can be rearranged to make a word meaning

   A  to give up under pressure
   B  the feeling or state of being angry
   C  extremely unpleasant, revolting
   D  none of the above

© MR STEGGELS ADVANCED INSTRUCTION PTY LTD

6. Choose the word that best completes the sentence protective

   Sally was very _____ of her younger brother when he started school.

   A   incentive
   B   protective
   C   dedicated
   D   disgusted

7. The letters in **stiloholf** can be rearranged to make a word meaning

   A   low mountains or low hills at the bottom of a larger mountain
   B   spread over a large area
   C   almost
   D   used before one fact that makes another fact surprising

8. Which word should replace the words in bold in the following sentence?

   Sharon smiled **in a way to intentionally keep something** when I asked where she lived.

   A   spluttering
   B   obviously
   C   coyly
   D   drastically

9. Choose the best word to complete the sentence

   This species of butterfly has _____ markings on its wings.

   A   distinct
   B   lavish
   C   developed
   D   colourless

10. What is the meaning of **parallel**?

    A   a type of flat shape with four equal straight sides
    B   a two dimensional shape
    C   along the plane of the horizon, at right angles to vertical
    D   the distance between lines is the same all along their length

© MR STEGGELS ADVANCED INSTRUCTION PTY LTD

11. Which word is both a verb (action) and a noun (a thing)?

    A   cartwheel
    B   refrigerate
    C   glace
    D   murky

12. Choose the word that best completes the sentence

    The _____ tornado was a disaster for the _____.

    A   devastating     region
    B   billowing       destination
    C   gigantic        resistance
    D   breakneck       motorway

13. Which word means **preserved in liquid sugar and then dried**?

    A   lavish
    B   gossamer
    C   glace
    D   none of the above

14. Which word is closest in meaning to **coax**?

    A   express
    B   persuade
    C   shake
    D   suggest

15. A first born child is often described as being the parents'

    A   affair
    B   territory
    C   pride and joy
    D   kiddo

© MR STEGGELS ADVANCED INSTRUCTION PTY LTD

16. Choose the word that best completes the sentence

My parents were furious when my sister ran away to join a _____ circus.

- A    fare
- B    Dutch
- C    travelling
- D    flywire

---

17. The letters in **eoeatrdc** can be rearranged to make a word meaning

- A    a small house in the country, used especially by people on holiday or taking part in sports
- B    to make a place more attractive
- C    boring, especially in appearance; having little colour and excitement
- D    extremely unpleasant

---

18. Food that has been **changed into substances that the body can use** is best described as

- A    dislodged
- B    abundant
- C    deposed
- D    digested

---

19. Choose the best meaning of **torture**

- A    to give up under pressure; surrender
- B    very harmful and able to cause illness or death
- C    the feeling or state of being angry
- D    a very unpleasant experience

---

20. Which word **describes the physical processes of the earth that reveal its origin and history**?

- A    geological
- B    crevasse
- C    expedition
- D    experiment

© MR STEGGELS ADVANCED INSTRUCTION PTY LTD

Solutions

## Unit 1

### Definitions

| 1 | dripping | 5 | glace | 9 | distinct | 13 | torture |
|---|---|---|---|---|---|---|---|
| 2 | misfortune | 6 | quiver | 10 | coax | 14 | refrigerate |
| 3 | lodge | 7 | poisonous | 11 | postpone | 15 | decorate |
| 4 | miserable | 8 | moderate | 12 | parliament | 16 | cartwheel |

### Word usage

| 1 | parliament | 5 | refrigerate | 9 | lodge | 13 | glace |
|---|---|---|---|---|---|---|---|
| 2 | distinct | 6 | decorate | 10 | dripping | 14 | miserable |
| 3 | poisonous | 7 | misfortune | 11 | quiver | 15 | moderate |
| 4 | torture | 8 | postpone | 12 | coax | 16 | cartwheel |

## Unit 2

### Definitions

| 1 | stubby | 5 | accent | 9 | moral | 13 | drab |
|---|---|---|---|---|---|---|---|
| 2 | territory | 6 | passage | 10 | vocalise | 14 | aquatic |
| 3 | suppressed | 7 | gross | 11 | secretion | 15 | visual pollution |
| 4 | scrawl | 8 | rip-off | 12 | gawking | 16 | slunk |

### Word usage

| 1 | slunk | 5 | drab | 9 | rip-off | 13 | gross |
|---|---|---|---|---|---|---|---|
| 2 | aquatic | 6 | accent | 10 | stubby | 14 | moral |
| 3 | visual pollution | 7 | suppressed | 11 | secretion | 15 | vocalise |
| 4 | gawking | 8 | territory | 12 | scrawl | 16 | passage |

## Unit 3

### Definitions

| 1 | foothills | 5 | petition | 9 | hardened | 13 | discoveries |
|---|---|---|---|---|---|---|---|
| 2 | billowing | 6 | virtually | 10 | annoyance | 14 | intact |
| 3 | eccentricity | 7 | timber | 11 | spluttering | 15 | coyly |
| 4 | whimper | 8 | in spite | 12 | expedition | 16 | foghorn |

## Unit 3

### Word usage

| 1 | foothills | 5 | spluttering | 9 | eccentricity | 13 | petition |
|---|---|---|---|---|---|---|---|
| 2 | whimper | 6 | billowing | 10 | annoyance | 14 | timber |
| 3 | virtually | 7 | coyly | 11 | discoveries | 15 | hardened |
| 4 | foghorn | 8 | in spite | 12 | intact | 16 | expedition |

## Unit 4

### Definitions

| 1 | crevasse | 5 | gigantic | 9 | yield | 13 | friction |
|---|---|---|---|---|---|---|---|
| 2 | experiment | 6 | inhospitable | 10 | empire | 14 | granite |
| 3 | lever | 7 | granary | 11 | presto | 15 | colourless |
| 4 | geological | 8 | rations | 12 | dynasty | 16 | pioneer |

### Word usage

| 1 | dynasty | 5 | inhospitable | 9 | friction | 13 | pioneer |
|---|---|---|---|---|---|---|---|
| 2 | crevasse | 6 | granary | 10 | yield | 14 | colourless |
| 3 | geological | 7 | empire | 11 | experiment | 15 | presto |
| 4 | rations | 8 | gigantic | 12 | lever | 16 | granite |

## Unit 5

### Definitions

| 1 | amid | 5 | exports | 9 | tournament | 13 | proclaim |
|---|---|---|---|---|---|---|---|
| 2 | steers | 6 | abandon | 10 | admiration | 14 | hexagonal |
| 3 | despise | 7 | protestor | 11 | underway | 15 | horizontal |
| 4 | corral | 8 | fare | 12 | rhomboid | 16 | parallel |

### Word usage

| 1 | horizontal | 5 | hexagonal | 9 | abandon | 13 | steers |
|---|---|---|---|---|---|---|---|
| 2 | tournament | 6 | rhomboid | 10 | underway | 14 | proclaim |
| 3 | parallel | 7 | fare | 11 | admiration | 15 | protestor |
| 4 | despise | 8 | corral | 12 | exports | 16 | amid |

© MR STEGGELS ADVANCED INSTRUCTION PTY LTD

# Unit 6

## Definitions

| 1 | enhance | 5 | breakneck | 9 | lyrics | 13 | semi-precious |
|---|---|---|---|---|---|---|---|
| 2 | motorway | 6 | part-time | 10 | campaign | 14 | bellowed |
| 3 | supposed | 7 | plague | 11 | records | 15 | deposed |
| 4 | dreary | 8 | poked | 12 | destination | 16 | diehard |

## Word usage

| 1 | enhance | 5 | diehard | 9 | lyrics | 13 | semi-precious |
|---|---|---|---|---|---|---|---|
| 2 | part-time | 6 | supposed | 10 | deposed | 14 | motorway |
| 3 | dreary | 7 | plague | 11 | campaign | 15 | destination |
| 4 | bellowed | 8 | poked | 12 | records | 16 | breakneck |

# Unit 7

## Definitions

| 1 | dew | 5 | lantern | 9 | scoundrel | 13 | oafish |
|---|---|---|---|---|---|---|---|
| 2 | gorgeous | 6 | budget | 10 | Dutch | 14 | pitch |
| 3 | gossamer | 7 | kiddo | 11 | broadcast | 15 | thundercloud |
| 4 | quilt | 8 | sapphire | 12 | insist | 16 | commentator |

## Word usage

| 1 | oafish | 5 | thundercloud | 9 | commentator | 13 | budget |
|---|---|---|---|---|---|---|---|
| 2 | Dutch | 6 | lantern | 10 | dew | 14 | broadcast |
| 3 | sapphire | 7 | quilt | 11 | pitch | 15 | gorgeous |
| 4 | scoundrel | 8 | gossamer | 12 | insist | 16 | kiddo |

# Unit 8

## Definitions

| 1 | lavish | 5 | renowned | 9 | Asia-Pacific | 13 | hoarding |
|---|---|---|---|---|---|---|---|
| 2 | attic | 6 | incentive | 10 | minister | 14 | harpsichord |
| 3 | discipline | 7 | region | 11 | resistance | 15 | disgusted |
| 4 | guillotine | 8 | loft | 12 | chameleon | 16 | affair |

© MR STEGGELS ADVANCED INSTRUCTION PTY LTD

# Unit 8

## Word usage

| 1 | chameleon | 5 | loft | 9 | disgusted | 13 | resistance |
| 2 | discipline | 6 | minister | 10 | harpsichord | 14 | guillotine |
| 3 | incentive | 7 | attic | 11 | hoarding | 15 | lavish |
| 4 | renowned | 8 | affair | 12 | region | 16 | Asia-Pacific |

# Unit 9

## Definitions

| 1 | dedicated | 5 | murky | 9 | series | 13 | barriers |
| 2 | protective | 6 | obviously | 10 | ventilation | 14 | scramble |
| 3 | engineering | 7 | translated | 11 | travelling | 15 | banned |
| 4 | upturned | 8 | freight | 12 | route | 16 | devote |

## Word usage

| 1 | dedicated | 5 | travelling | 9 | upturned | 13 | route |
| 2 | translated | 6 | obviously | 10 | scrambled | 14 | banned |
| 3 | murky | 7 | barriers | 11 | engineering | 15 | protective |
| 4 | series | 8 | devote | 12 | ventilation | 16 | freight |

# Unit 10

## Definitions

| 1 | pride and joy | 5 | glinting | 9 | dislodged | 13 | paralysis |
| 2 | fasting | 6 | drastically | 10 | fluorescent | 14 | devastating |
| 3 | abundant | 7 | flywire | 11 | cells | 15 | obese |
| 4 | toxin | 8 | antidote | 12 | developed | 16 | digest |

## Word usage

| 1 | cells | 5 | pride and joy | 9 | paralysis | 13 | developed |
| 2 | dislodged | 6 | drastically | 10 | glinting | 14 | obese |
| 3 | fasting | 7 | toxin | 11 | fluorescent | 15 | flywire |
| 4 | abundant | 8 | antidote | 12 | devastating | 16 | digest |

© MR STEGGELS ADVANCED INSTRUCTION PTY LTD

# Test 1 solutions

| Q | A | Notes |
|---|---|---|
| 1 | C | **accent** refers to the way in which people in a particular area pronounce words |
| 2 | D | **amid** means in the middle of or surrounded by |
| 3 | A | to **fare** is to succeed or to **perform** in a stated way in a particular situation |
| 4 | C | the opposite of **murky** is **clear** |
| 5 | B | **droelsunc** → **scoundrel** a person, especially a man, who treats other people very badly |
| 6 | A | The tiny boat was **upturned** by a large wave. |
| 7 | D | **taaunndb** → **adundant** available in large quantities so that there is more than enough |
| 8 | A | **devote** and **dedicate** mean to give time, energy and resources to someone or something |
| 9 | C | **yield** means to give in or surrender; **resist** means to fight against |
| 10 | D | Jim **despised** Adam after he stole his expensive bike and sold it for $50. |
| 11 | D | a **sapphire** is bright blue; **granite** is grey, pink or black; **gossamer** is very light and delicate |
| 12 | D | A **tournament** is a **competition** for teams or single players in which a series of games is played, and the winners of each game play against each other until only one winner is left |
| 13 | A | **lyrics** are the words of a song |
| 14 | B | a **moral** is a **message** about how you should or should not behave |
| 15 | C | He drove down the **motorway** at **breakneck** speed. |
| 16 | B | The **loft** was directly above and behind the kitchen and with no privacy screen, so it wasn't the best place for a bedroom. |
| 17 | C | **rodserc** → **records** the best or fastest things ever done |
| 18 | C | **territory** and **region** refer to areas of land |
| 19 | B | **eccentricity** means the state of being strange or unusual, in a humorous way |
| 20 | D | The bus followed a **route** on its way from the city to the beach. |

© MR STEGGELS ADVANCED INSTRUCTION PTY LTD

# Test 2 solutions

| Q | A | Notes |
|---|---|---|
| 1 | B | **secretion** refers to liquid produced by an animal or plant |
| 2 | A | **intact** means complete and in the original state |
| 3 | D | **gawking** means **staring** at someone or something in a rude or stupid way |
| 4 | C | **gigantic** means huge in scale; **stubby** means short and thick |
| 5 | B | **slecouorsl** → **colourless** not exciting or interesting |
| 6 | D | **Fluorescent** lights are very bright so they are often used in offices. |
| 7 | D | **yaanrrg** → **granary** a building for storing grain |
| 8 | A | **drab** and **dreary** mean lacking colour and vitality |
| 9 | C | an **antidote** stops the effects of a **poison** |
| 10 | D | Our teacher offered free time as **incentive** to work harder. |
| 11 | A | **In spite** of our best efforts, we have been unable to contact the winner of last week's lottery. |
| 12 | D | a **chameleon** is a lizard that can change its skin colour according to its environment |
| 13 | C | **drastically** means in a way that is extreme and sudden |
| 14 | D | **gross** means extremely unpleasant |
| 15 | B | A, C and D are mathematical terms; **lever** is not |
| 16 | B | It would be hours before the **freight** reached its **destination**. |
| 17 | C | **bndean** → **banned** not allowed |
| 18 | D | **underway** means happening now; **postponed** means put off until a later time |
| 19 | C | a **guillotine** is a device, invented in France, consisting of a sharp blade in a tall frame used to remove someone's head |
| 20 | B | India was ruled by a **dynasty** started by the Mogul family. |

© MR STEGGELS ADVANCED INSTRUCTION PTY LTD

# Test 3 solutions

| Q | A | Notes |
|---|---|---|
| 1 | B | **presto** means fast tempo |
| 2 | D | **ventilation** means the movement of fresh air around a closed space |
| 3 | D | **obviously** means in a way that is easy to understand or clear to see |
| 4 | A | **renowned** means **famous**; unknown is the opposite |
| 5 | D | **oafish** means stupid, rude or awkward |
| 6 | B | When the bell went, the students **scrambled** out of the classroom. |
| 7 | A | **canehen → enhance** to improve the quality, amount, or strength of something |
| 8 | C | Sir Isaac Newton was a **pioneer** in the field of science. |
| 9 | C | Red blood **cells** remove carbon dioxide from your body. |
| 10 | B | The explorers set out on an **expedition** across Red Mountain. |
| 11 | D | To my great **annoyance**, the roast dinner I had ordered was served cold. |
| 12 | C | a **toxin** is poisonous substance that causes **diseases** |
| 13 | A | a **rhomboid** is a type of flat shape with four equal straight sides |
| 14 | C | **visual pollution** is the presence of any unwanted sight that can ruin the appeal of an area |
| 15 | D | **granite** is a hard grey, pink or black rock used in building or monuments |
| 16 | A | He was in the **corral**, teaching his new horse to jump. |
| 17 | B | **loveeeddp → developed** one of the rich countries of the world |
| 18 | D | a **petition** is a document signed by a large number of people demanding or asking for some action from the government. A **protestor** shows that they disagree with something by standing somewhere, shouting and carrying signs. |
| 19 | C | **plague** means to cause worry or difficulty to someone over a period of time |
| 20 | D | The wet weather is **miserable** for all of the children at camp. |

© MR STEGGELS ADVANCED INSTRUCTION PTY LTD

# Test 4 solutions

| Q | A | Notes |
|---|---|---|
| 1 | A | **suppressed** means prevented something from being seen or expressed |
| 2 | C | **slunk** means walked away from somewhere quietly and unnoticed |
| 3 | D | **freight** and **exports** are terms used to describe products that are sold to another country |
| 4 | B | **paralysis** means the loss of the ability to **move** all or part of your body |
| 5 | C | The **tournament** had to be **postponed** due to poor weather. |
| 6 | C | He was **proclaimed** king after the death of his father, Barnaby VII. |
| 7 | A | resets → **steers** young male cattle that have had their sex organs removed, usually kept for meat |
| 8 | C | The general will lead a **campaign** to take control of enemy states by force. |
| 9 | D | **barriers** means fences or walls that stop people from going somewhere |
| 10 | B | The active volcano made the region **inhospitable**. |
| 11 | C | a **crevasse** is a deep, narrow opening or crack in an area of thick ice or rock |
| 12 | A | **engineering** is the work in designing and building machines and structures, and the **study** of this |
| 13 | C | **friction** is the **force** that makes it difficult for one object to slide along the surface of another |
| 14 | C | The scientists will conduct **an experiment** for the purpose of discovering more about gravity. |
| 15 | D | a **diehard** is someone who is unwilling to change their support even when many others disagree |
| 16 | D | When war broke out, **rations were** reduced and many people went hungry. |
| 17 | C | dopseed → **deposed** removed someone important from a powerful position |
| 18 | A | a **budget** is the amount of money you have available to spend |
| 19 | D | a **lever** is a bar or handle that moves around a point, so that one end of it can be pushed or pulled; a **wheelbarrow** is an example of a lever |
| 20 | B | The New Year celebrations get **underway** at 9pm with the kids' fireworks display. |

© MR STEGGELS ADVANCED INSTRUCTION PTY LTD

# Test 5 solutions

| Q | A | Notes |
|---|---|---|
| 1 | A | **supposed** means to have a duty or a responsibility to do something |
| 2 | C | **poked** means pushed a finger quickly into someone or something |
| 3 | D | **hoarding** is collecting large amounts of something to keep in a safe, often secret, place |
| 4 | C | **fasting** is eating little or no food for a period of time |
| 5 | D | **soorugge → gorgeous** very beautiful |
| 6 | B | Sally was very **protective** of her younger brother when he started school. |
| 7 | A | **stiloholf → foothills** low mountains or low hills at the bottom of a larger mountain |
| 8 | C | Sharon smiled **coyly** when I asked her if she knew who had stolen my money. |
| 9 | A | This species of butterfly has **distinct** markings on its wings. |
| 10 | D | **parallel** means that the distance between lines is the same all along their length |
| 11 | A | **cartwheel** (verb) a fast skilful movement of the body in a sideways somersault, like a wheel <br> **cartwheel** (noun) the wheel of a cart |
| 12 | A | The **devastating** tornado was a disaster for the **region**. |
| 13 | C | **glace** means preserved in liquid sugar and then dried |
| 14 | B | **coax** means to **persuade** someone gently to do something |
| 15 | C | a first born child is often described as being someone that the parents are very proud of → their **pride and joy** |
| 16 | C | My parents were upset when my sister ran away to join a **travelling** circus. |
| 17 | B | **eoeatrdc → decorate** to make a place more attractive |
| 18 | D | **digested** means changed food that you have eaten into substances that your body can use |
| 19 | D | **torture** means a very unpleasant experience |
| 20 | A | **geological** describes the physical processes of the earth that reveal its origin and history |

www.ingramcontent.com/pod-product-compliance
Lightning Source LLC
LaVergne TN
LVHW061318060426
835507LV00019B/2214